GW01246863

Index

Aberdeen Angus	2
Angel in Disguise	3
Best foot forward	8
Brief Encounter	10
Connections	12
Daily Bread	15
Eric	16
Fresh Start	17
Gooseberries	20
Jerry the builder	22
Keep Right On	24
Passing through	30
Side Effects	32
Sunrise on Shoreham Beach	34
Wimbledon Fortnight	36

201007647

Aberdeen Angus

Angus is a Scotsman who lives in Aberdeen,
And never does anything rash,
He hotly denies that he's ever been mean,
Just prefers to hold on to his cash.

He's canny and careful, and cautious as well
As prudent in counting the cost
Of his shares, in deciding to buy or to sell
To make a tax gain or tax loss.

He has a dear wife he calls "My sweet Jean"
Who enjoys going out to the shops,
In the granite city of great Aberdeen
Retail therapy's close to the top.

Angus cannot deny that though close to his heart,
He loves Jean a little bit less
When the bills come in, and he's forced to part
With his money, which causes him stress.

But he says even this cannot mar married bliss,
In new clothes Jean's a wonderful sight,
As she cuddles up close and gives him a kiss
He succumbs to her charms with delight.

Angel in Disguise

The eyes of the ethereal messenger followed me as I moved around the room. A beautiful specimen of naked young manhood, I wasn't sure if he was a human or angelic being. His arms were open wide as if to invite people to approach for a blessing. In fairytale woodland setting reminiscent of *A Midsummer Night's Dream,* the moonlight shone behind him radiating out to the world. Open and innocent, there was such a magnetic quality about him that I kept returning to have another look. I was thankful that I was alone, and had time to spare and no one waiting to hurry me along to the next room in the gallery.

I was trying to mentally work out what the painter had intended his message to be, when I thought I could smell smoke and the silence was shattered by a fire alarm. People appeared as if from nowhere, running in all directions. My mind raced with possibilities, fire, a terrorist bomb, or just a smoke alarm in the nearby café, as I too raced towards the nearest exit. The bell was interrupted by a loudspeaker system announcing over and over again, "Do not panic. Do not use the lifts. Proceed to the nearest fire exit."

Although everything seemed to fast forward from that moment, my later memories were all in slow motion. The entrance to the stairwell was jammed with people trying to push past a young mother with a crying baby and toddler in a double buggy. A middle-aged woman with an elderly man in a wheelchair were thrust in a corner as the more able-bodied tried to squeeze through in their hurry to get out. We could smell the smoke strongly now and it was becoming harder to breathe freely.

A young girl started to scream hysterically and an old man tried to use his stick as a battering ram, but as congestion built up we felt a surge from adjoining stairways pressing in on us and we made no progress. A fat red-faced man swore repeatedly, and I put an arm round a tiny, elderly, stick-thin woman next to me who was shaking uncontrollably. In the midst of the panic I noticed the extraordinary sight of a middle-aged couple who were standing with their backs against the wall, seemingly totally unperturbed, continuing to read from paperback books they had extracted from their bags.

Seemingly out of nowhere a voice of authority from above said calmly, "Stand aside please" and two firemen appeared, one picking up the buggy, and the other the occupant of the wheelchair.

As they descended, people were parting to let them through the centre, like the dividing of the Red Sea. They were followed by two others from the floor above, one supporting a young man, chalk white and gasping for breath, the other cradling a black curly headed baby. Now subdued, we followed them outside onto the pavement.

As we emerged unscathed into the sunlight, we started to laugh and talk to complete strangers as if we had known each other all our lives. I noticed four fire engines, two or more ambulances and several police cars parked in puddles in the road. A man in a pin-striped suit was talking rapidly into his mobile phone, a child sobbed for her teddy, and the woman who had kept tight hold of my arm whispered to me, "It brings back memories of people crowding into the underground shelters during the Blitz." I handed her over to paramedics who were moving amongst the crowd to see if we were hurt or suffering from shock. Then a policeman with a loud hailer was dispersing the crowd and we were moved on.

Later, curled up on the sofa at home, with a glass of wine in my hand, my partner Mike and I watched the news, and there was a short clip about the fire which had been rapidly brought under control by the firefighting teams. The report said that there were minor casualties and some damage to paintings, also that arson could not be ruled out, and a forensic team was investigating.

Mike's face was crumpled with concern as he said, "You're always so outwardly calm Emma, but I bet you were scared underneath weren't you?"

"Just a bit," I admitted, "but those firemen were great, like angels in disguise."

"Pretty hefty angels," he snorted, "I thought they were supposed to be delicate with halos and wings" and my mind went back to the gallery and my ethereal messenger. I wondered how many of the paintings had been damaged, and if he had survived. It suddenly seemed tremendously important that he, in particular, should have escaped the fire.

When it reopened, I visited the gallery and made my way to the third floor. Straight away I noticed the empty space and felt a disproportionate sense of loss. I went up to an attendant, described the painting and asked if he knew what had happened to it.

"I'm new on this job I'm afraid," he said, "but if you go to the Enquiry Desk and ask for Bill, he'll be able to tell you."

I tracked Bill down on the Ground Floor. "Yes miss," he said, "there's a tale to tell about that picture. When the fire started a young man, stark naked, was reportedly seen, shepherding anyone who was lost or unable to help themselves towards the fire exits. The strange thing was," he said, warming to his theme, "he was evidently seen on all four floors at the same time."

"How amazing," I said politely, not sure if I believed a word of it, "but how about the picture?"

"Well I was coming to that," Bill said, relishing his story. "If you follow me I'll show you."

He took me down to the basement, where several pictures were awaiting restoration. The picture was propped up on an easel in the centre, completely undamaged, except for one thing. Where the body of my ethereal messenger had been there was now a totally blank space.

First published by Pedestal Magazine

Best Foot Forward

"Put your best foot forward," my mother used to say,
While I meandered dreamily as if I had all day
To do this and that and other things that needed to be
done,
None of which I'd estimate was any kind of fun.

"Put your best foot forward" my sister used to say,
"We'll be late, there is no time for us to stop and
play,
I know your legs are shorter but you really must keep
up,
Not wander off to climb the trees or pick a
buttercup."

"Put your best foot forward" they said to me at
school
We marched in order of our height, I felt an utter
fool,
I was tiny for my age, had not grown very fast,
But Barbara was smaller and always came in last.

"Put your best foot forward," my husband said to me,
"You need to keep alert and keen when going out to
sea
I know sights are spectacular when we are in the
boat,
But drifting into daydreams will not keep us afloat."

"Put your best foot forward," my grandson skips ahead,
I follow in his footsteps but with a slower tread.
"Come on Grandma please keep up, this is so much fun."
I answer him quite firmly "Grandmas do not run."

Brief Encounter

"Hallo Wendy. How are you? You haven't changed a bit."

Wendy looked carefully at the slightly stooped, balding figure of the man standing directly in her path outside the supermarket. A vague memory stirred, but no name surfaced. She smiled brightly "I'm very well thanks, and you?"

"Apart from the odd twinge, I'm very fit. How are all your family? Your brother John, is he still in the police force? And your sister Sarah, did she ever recover from her car accident? The last time I saw her she was in a wheelchair"

'This is getting worse' Wendy thought. 'He not only remembers me but John and Sarah as well.'

"John is fine, he's a detective inspector now and Sarah recovered well thank you. She's a grandmother of three. What about you?" Wendy said, desperately hoping for a clue.

"You remember Marcia of course, the girl I married." He frowned slightly and lowered his voice. "Nothing was ever the same after we split up

Wendy. You were always the real love of my life. Remember the moonlight picnics on the beach, skinny dipping at midnight, walking home arms entwined as the dawn broke?"

"Oh yes." As memory came flooding back, Wendy caught a glimpse of a slim dark haired boy in the twinkling eyes of the rotund figure facing her. "Tom. How could I forget?"

At that moment a strident voice broke through their reverie. "Thomas. Where have you been? I've done all the shopping. The least you can do is put it in the car."

Tom visibly shrank as the light went from his eyes "Yes dear, straight away." He shuffled guiltily after the trolley, just raising his hand slightly as he whispered goodbye.

Connections

The lift creaked, shuddered, and then ground to a halt between the first and second floors of the Sunny View Care Home for the elderly.

Ellie looked at her watch "Oh No! Now I'll be late picking up the kids from school."

She pressed the red alarm button and took her mobile phone out of her bag. The lift, like the residents of the Home, looked as if it had seen better days. She wasn't sure if it was a good or bad thing that there were no other occupants. She punched in her friend Kate's number to ask her to hold on to Sam and Becky till she got home. 'No signal.' Ellie punched the red button again.

Starting to panic she addressed God. "I don't know if You are listening up there but this is absolutely unfair. I go out of my way to do a good turn and visit Great Aunt Mary. I let her ramble on because she's lonely, so I'm already late for the children and now you do *this.*"

Resorting to a keep Ellie calm strategy she started to plan the evening's menu. *Not sausage and mash or fish and chips we've had those already this week. No time to get to the shops.*

There's pasta and sauce in the cupboard. That will have to do, with ice cream for afters.

She wondered how long she would have to wait before rescue came, and her mind went back to her days in her very first job as a telephonist at a lift company. The engineers would phone in to check on emergencies and she would give them details of any calls that came in. She remembered how they used to joke and tell her to give the caller reassurance that they were on their way, adding "Just leave out that as it's lunch time, we're stopping off at the pub for a bite on the way." She used to laugh along with them specially when Jake phoned in. He was the youngest and would chat her up on the phone, regardless of the fact that there were three old ladies stuck in a lift between floors at Debenhams.

Wondering how she could have been so heartless, her mind jerked back to the present. She sent up another prayer that she wouldn't be stuck for much longer, and that Kate would step in for the children, when the lift started to shake and judder again and gradually move downwards to the sound of voices calling up that rescue was at hand.

Relieved beyond measure, as the doors opened at Ground Floor level, she was greeted by three engineers ready to help her out. "Didn't think we'd abandon you, did you love? "One asked. "Got here quick as we could."

Ellie looked Jake straight in the eye and said. "Are you sure about that?"

Daily Bread

Cereals for breakfast or shall we have brunch?
Sausages for supper, sandwiches for lunch.

Cake in the oven, coffee in the cup,
Must do the shopping, we need to stock up.

Food in the cupboard, petrol in the tank,
Bills paid up-to-date, money in the bank.

Roast beef on Sunday or shall we have pork?
Sitting round the table, family can talk.

Start again on Monday with bubble and squeak,
Potato, cabbage, onion, and I'll add a leek,

Friends to meet, a place to go, at night a bed,
Books to read, our space, a roof over our head.

So we pray each day, "Give us our daily bread,"
That we may in every way continue to be fed.

Eric

Has anyone here met Eric?
I hear that he's moved in quite near
The Shepherd and Dog, and that he reeks
Of tobacco, old socks and stale beer.

Has anyone spoken to Eric?
Or has the smell put you all off?
I gather it's hard to hear what he says
Through the wheeze, and the smoker's cough.

What do we know about Eric?
His family background, his past,
Or do we just see what he seems to be,
A shambles, a mess, an outcast?

Has anyone guessed whether Eric's
A drunk, or drug addict, or worse,
Been mentally ill, in prison maybe,
A drain on the public purse?

But someone's found out about Eric
And turned these ideas upside down,
For he's a war hero with medals galore
Eric's a man of renown.

Fresh Start

Jack clutched Fraser Bear firmly in one hand, keeping an eye on the bag at his feet. He'd remembered to put in the Harry Potter DVD, a parting present from Auntie and Uncle at his last foster home.

Pete, his key worker was chatting as he drove. Jack wasn't sure what a key worker did. *Perhaps he's good at getting different keys to work,* he thought as he looked at Pete's bunch attached to the ring on his car key.

"You'll like Terry and Angela" Pete was saying. "They have two boys of their own so you will have friends to play with"

Terry and Angela, not Auntie and Uncle this time, Jack thought, wondering if the other boys were bigger or smaller than him. As he remembered some of the boys from the Childrens' Home where he'd stayed before Auntie and Uncle, he clutched Fraser Bear closer to him and his thumb on the other hand went into his mouth.

"Not far now" Pete said breezily, noticing the thumb. "The twins are smaller than you, so you will be the biggest. I've told Terry and Angela you're good with younger ones so they'll be glad to have you aboard."

Taking his thumb out Jack asked "Do they live on a boat?"

Pete laughed "No, that's just an expression. They live in a house, and you will have your own room."

They drew up outside a large semi-detached house in a tree lined road, and as Pete got out of the car, a large man with a booming voice came forward to greet them, closely followed by a slim fair haired woman and two boys of about four, who Jack thought looked exactly the same, each with a shock of untidy red hair.

As he shrank back in his seat, his thumb crept back into his mouth, but Angela came forward, and with a firm gesture to Terry and the boys to keep back, came up to the car. "Don't worry about them Jack, they're just excited to meet you. Come on in and I'll show you round. Is that your bear? Does he have a name?"

"Fraser Bear," Jack answered, looking into Angela's face. Her smile went right across her face and into her eyes.

"Well I expect Fraser Bear is ready for his tea, so you'd better bring him in," she said. "What's in the bag?"

"My Harry Potter DVD, my clothes, and," his lip trembled, "my special scrap book with a photo of Mummy."

"Well this is your home now, you'll have your very own room, and you can put your things wherever you want and they will be quite safe." Adding under her breath, "And so my little one will you."

Bending down she took Jack's hand and led him into the house.

Gooseberries

"I can see it now," he said.
"A green cover, with
'Gooseberries' on the front.
A worthy successor to 'Raspberries.'
Part of a fruit collection."

So I thought of gooseberries,
lip-puckeringly tart,
juicy, full-flavoured,
more rarely seen than other fruits
except in fools.

I searched the internet.
Found out about
babies discovered under bushes,
and unwelcome third parties
intruding on lovers' meetings,
and shared that with him.

"Roast duck, or goose, or fish
with gooseberry sauce," he said,
"would make a nice change."

I learned how gooseberries
look like clementines
that had never grown,
and their relatives are currants.

"Crumbles, tarts or pies"
he mused.

"Did you know," I asked
"that a silly goose is
someone stupid?
Geese lack intellect,
and 'green as gooseberries'
can have a double meaning?"

"All this talk of food is
making me hungry," he replied,
"Do we have any plans for dinner?"

"Not yet"
I answered.

"I suppose," he said,
"you could always make me a fool."

Jerry the Builder

Jerry the builder was jack of all trades
Regretfully master of none,
His advert laid claim to a number of skills
Passed down from father to son.

When fitting some windows in tailor made frames
His expertise none could surpass.
The trouble arose when the owner found out
Jerry'd ordered the wrong kind of glass.

In carpentry work Jerry took a great pride,
With chisel and hammer and saw,
But trouble arose when he found on the plan
A window instead of a door.

When roofing he was right on top of the world,
Gave passers-by all his best smiles,
Progress was good till he'd got half way through
And found he'd run right out of tiles.

As a plumber he knew he would always have work
With bathrooms and kitchens and sinks,
But he came unstuck when the drains all blocked up
And the neighbours created a stink.

With fencing he reckoned he couldn't go wrong,
Fence panels came ready to fix,
But checking the order he found that instead
Of sixty, he'd ordered just six.

Jerry the builder was jack of all trades
Regretfully master of none,
He's now learned a lesson which he passes on
"Don't ever cut corners my son."

Keep Right On

Maud Jenkins sat back in her chair with a sigh of contentment, a cup of tea and chocolate digestive biscuit on the table on one side and her zimmer frame ready at hand on the other. She felt her usual sense of achievement, having negotiated her trip to the post office to collect her pension, and then on to the village store to stock up on groceries now neatly packed away in her kitchen. She checked again her pension money laid out in neat piles on the table to cover all her outgoings for the week ahead.

Of course she couldn't have managed it all without Lenny's help. Her grandson came every week to give her a hand with the shopping. She always tried to give him something, but he refused every time saying, "Aw, Nan I don't want yer money," and then with a grin, "You keep it fer yer old age."

With five grown sons living nearby with their families she knew that help was always at hand, but she wanted to be independent and stay in her own home as long as she possibly could. She looked around at the family photos which covered every available space on her dresser, wondering where she would put the latest addition, a six week old great granddaughter.

The intercom which connected her retirement flat to the main door buzzed, startling her out of her reverie. Her family all knew the key code so it couldn't be any of them. She got up stiffly and went to the door of her flat. "Who is it?"

"Hello luv. Just come to check the gas." A man's voice crackled slightly from outside.

"Oh right. Come on up." Maud pressed the button on the intercom and opened the door to her flat. Seconds later she heard the whirring of the lift and two young men came in, one of them flashing an identity card at her.

"Jim here will just check your meter, missis. Won't take a minute. Nice place you got here. What a lot of photos. All your family?"

"Yes." With one hand on her frame she picked up one photo after another, answering his questions and showing off the one in the centre of her granddaughter, Louise, with her mortar board and gown when she'd graduated from University.

"They call it Uni, now," she said, just as Jim came back into the room.

"All done Missis. We'll leave you in peace." As he said that Jim's eye went to the pension money on the table and, quick as a flash, he scooped it into his right pocket.

"Oh no you don't!" Maud was standing between him and the door and as he side-stepped to get round her, lashed out with her frame and caught him on his left ankle. He fell awkwardly to the floor, jewellery spilling out of his other pocket. His mate moved in on her other side and swept the frame from under her, so she fell against the table knocking her head on the corner as she went down.

When she came round the flat was empty and she was lying on the carpet with blood from her forehead dripping into her eye. As memory returned she tried to get up, but she was hurting all over and thought something might be broken. She fumbled at her cardigan, found her community alarm button and pressed it with trembling hands.

A voice came on her speaker phone. "Mrs Jenkins. Can you hear this? What help do you need? Are you unwell? Can you reach the phone?"

Maud turned her head towards the phone which at the moment looked to be far above her and a long way away. She pressed the button again and cried for help as loudly as she could.

The voice came again. "Mrs Jenkins. Help is on the way. We've alerted the key holder. Hello Maud. Can you press the button again so that I know you've heard me?"

 The voice kept speaking to her as Maud weakly pressed the button again, but everything was swimming around her, and the rose pattern on the carpet seemed to be coming up to meet her.

After that everything happened very suddenly. The warden to the flats appeared and Brenda one of her daughters-in-law who had been alerted as a key holder. Two paramedics arrived and she was gently lifted into an ambulance.

 "She'll need stitches in that head wound," she heard one say. "And x-rays to make sure nothing's broken. They'll most likely keep her in. She must be suffering from shock after that fall"

Maud heard the word 'fall' and came round with a jolt. "I didn't fall. I was pushed. There were two men in my flat. I was robbed and mugged."

The paramedic suddenly looked at her intently. "What's that Mrs Jenkins?   Are you saying this wasn't an accident?"

"Of course not." Maud was indignant. "Two men. From the Gas they said. Took me jewellery and all me pension money. But I got one of them round the ankle with my frame. I brought him down," she added proudly.   "I was outnumbered. If there were only one I'd have stopped him getting away. You'd best get the police on the job. I can give a good description.   Maybe they'll put it on Crimewatch, and if they catch them it'll stop some poor old soul getting robbed. There are some got no family and can't stick up for themselves, you know."

By the time she reached the hospital, Maud was already starting to recover. After being patched up in A & E she only needed to be kept in for one night for observation, before being discharged to the care of her extended family. They took it in turns to have her to stay and made sure all her bills were paid up-to-date, until she was ready to return to her flat, which Lenny had redecorated in her absence.

The police had taken a description and done some forensic tests and said they would do everything they could, but Maud was disappointed that they said nothing about her appearing on "Crimewatch."

Four weeks later she was gently escorted in to her seniors' club by her community transport driver, where she displayed her now fading bruises and re-lived the tale of her ordeal to a rapt audience.

"You can't give up," she told them. "We learned that in the war. Otherwise that Hitler would have come in and walked all over us."

Passing Through

A new life born
dependent, trusting
others for every need,
food, clothing and cuddles.

Then a toddler,
terrible twos,

Passing through ...

To a life of learning
at school, teachers, friends.
Reading, writing, arithmetic,
scraped knees in the playground.

Now a teenager
with spots, talk of exams, and sex,

Passing through ...

To an adult life,
college, job, the world of work.
Finding a partner, falling in love,
leaving home, responsibilities,

Then a parent with
pain, joy, and sleepless nights,

Passing through ...

To middle age,
discover new interests and friends.
Mid-life crisis, an empty nest
as children find partners.

Now a grandparent,
surprised by joy, pleasure and pride,

Passing through ...

To retirement,
free prescriptions, pensions, bus passes,
pills and potions, treatments and therapies.
Memories surface from long ago.

Then the last journey,
leaving others to remember,
 who are also ...

Passing through

Side effects

I'm suffering from side effects
listed on the leaflet, enclosed
with my prescription tablets.

For a start I'm developing
a headache and nausea,
though that could be a result
of over indulgence on holiday.

Dizziness, light headedness
and mental confusion
are on the list,
and now in my head.

Bruising more easily
can be a side effect,
but I do bump into things.
Perhaps out of mental confusion
caused by the tablets.

I've never had mood alterations
or depression before,
but I notice while reading the list
that my mood is changing,
and I am becoming depressed.

As I read on
palpitations and rapid heart beat
are definitely overtaking me,
I think I am heading for a panic attack.

I'm suffering from weakness and fatigue,
maybe I should lie down for a while,
put the leaflet aside. . .

But keep on taking the tablets.

Sunrise on Shoreham Beach

The tide is out
as the sun rises
on Shoreham Beach.

I am alone.
The beach is mine.
Only one other
solitary dog walker
in the distance.

Ten minutes ago
the sky was still dark.
Now it blazes with
orange, red, and gold.
God's wake up call.

The moon not ready to retire
sits quietly in the west,
as a flock of gulls fly north
black against the sky.

The sea first dark,
then lit with reflected light,
turns grey and then blue
as the dawn colours fade.

The lights from boats
pair-trawling for fish
are now extinguished,
and the boats merge
into one on the horizon.

The tide turns to come in

Wimbledon Fortnight

Do not worry if I'm not polite,
The whites are on, the racquets out again,
Don't you know it's Wimbledon fortnight?

If you phone I may not sound too bright
Or focused on whatever you may say,
Do not worry if I'm not polite

No time to read and even less to write,
Housework and the washing are on hold,
Don't you know it's Wimbledon fortnight?

If you visit I'll keep out of sight
With curtains drawn and television on,
Do not worry if I'm not polite

With rain there was a window of respite,
But now they have a roof on centre court,
Don't you know it's Wimbledon fortnight?

Friends I pray you please do not take fright
If I am not around from noon till dusk,
Do not worry if I'm not polite,
Don't you know it's Wimbledon fortnight?

Made in the USA
Charleston, SC
25 May 2012